THE ORCHE

A Play by
JEAN ANOUILH

Translated by
MIRIAM JOHN

Samuel French - London
New York - Toronto - Hollywood

© 1967 by Jean Anouilh and Miriam John

Rights of Performance by Amateurs are controlled by Samuel French Ltd, 52 Fitzroy Street, London W1T 5JR, and they, or their authorized agents, issue licences to amateurs on payment of a fee. **It is an infringement of the Copyright to give any performance or public reading of the play before the fee has been paid and the licence issued.**
The Royalty Fee indicated below is subject to contract and subject to variation at the sole discretion of Samuel French Ltd.

Basic fee for each and every
performance by amateurs   Code F
in the British Isles

The publication of this play does not imply that it is necessarily available for performance by amateurs or professionals, either in the British Isles or Overseas. Amateurs and professionals considering a production are strongly advised in their own interests to apply to the appropriate agents for written consent before starting rehearsals or booking a theatre or hall.

ISBN 978 0 573 02343 9

Please see page iv for further copyright information

CHARACTERS:

Patricia, first violin
Pamela, second violin
Madame Hortense, double bass and leader of the
   orchestra
Suzanne Délicias, cello
Emmeline, viola
Léona, flute
Monsieur Léon, piano
Monsieur Lebonze, manager of the brasserie
The Waiter ⎫
The Doctor ⎭ non-acting

The action takes place on the platform of a spa town
brasserie

Time—the present

COPYRIGHT INFORMATION
(See also page ii)

This play is fully protected under the Copyright Laws of the British Commonwealth of Nations, the United States of America and all countries of the Berne and Universal Copyright Conventions.

All rights, including Stage, Motion Picture, Radio, Television, Public Reading, and Translation into Foreign Languages, are strictly reserved.

No part of this publication may lawfully be reproduced in ANY form or by any means — photocopying, typescript, recording (including video-recording), manuscript, electronic, mechanical, or otherwise — or be transmitted or stored in a retrieval system, without prior permission.

Licences are issued subject to the understanding that it shall be made clear in all advertising matter that the audience will witness an amateur performance; that the names of the authors of the plays shall be included on all announcements and on all programmes; and that the integrity of the authors' work will be preserved.

The Royalty Fee is subject to contract and subject to variation at the sole discretion of Samuel French Ltd.

In Theatres or Halls seating Four Hundred or more the fee will be subject to negotiation.

In Territories Overseas the fee quoted in this Acting Edition may not apply. A fee will be quoted on application to our local authorized agent, or if there is no such agent, on application to Samuel French Ltd, London.

VIDEO-RECORDING OF AMATEUR PRODUCTIONS

Please note that the copyright laws governing video-recording are extremely complex and that it should not be assumed that any play may be video-recorded for *whatever purpose* without first obtaining the permission of the appropriate agents. The fact that a play is published by Samuel French Ltd does not indicate that video rights are available or that Samuel French Ltd controls such rights.

MUSICAL NUMBERS

1. Lively piece (not specified)
2. *Impressions of Autumn* (Chandoisy)
3. "Cockades and Cock-crows" (*arr.* Benoisseau)
4. "Cuban Delights"

Suitable replacements may be made and the text altered accordingly, provided these are available in the necessary arrangements

THE ORCHESTRA

Sparkling music fro n behind the lowered Curtain, which then rises on an all-female orchestra on the platform of a spa town brasserie. The restaurant is not visible. The women are dressed in exactly similar bespangled black gowns with a single pink rose as ornament

At the piano, with his back to the audience, is a rather wan, skinny little man, hardly noticeable at first. To one side is a stand with a card bearing number three. The lively piece comes to an end shortly after Curtain rise. As soon as they finish playing, the musicians start talking

Patricia Then I add some shallots and leave it to marinate. Just two minutes—no longer. When I have my sauce ready, I cut the veal in small cubes . . .

Pamela I put bacon with mine.

Patricia For real *timbale Poitevine* you *never* use bacon, if you don't mind me saying so.

Pamela Well, I do, always.

Patricia (*thin-lipped*) Then it isn't *timbale Poitevine*, it's pig swill. I come from Loudun; I should know.

They hand their music sheets back to Madame Hortense, who plays double bass and is leader of the orchestra

Pamela Who's boasting? I come from Batignolles.

Patricia (*sourly*) Oh—Paris!

Madame Hortense, still gathering up music, is speaking to Suzanne Délicias, who is knitting quietly between pieces behind her cello. They are continuing a conversation

Madame Hortense Three plain, three purl, slip three, and the same again.

Suzanne Délicias That's Japanese stitch.

Madame Hortense No. Japanese stitch has a wrong side, my dear; this stitch has two sides.

Suzanne Délicias (*with a sour little laugh*) Excuse me, but if you loop it like that, your work has quite simply got two wrong sides! It must look horrible for a man's pull-over.

Madame Hortense Just as you like. Anyway, Japanese stitch looks vulgar.

Emmeline (*finishing a conversation with Léona, who is slightly hunchbacked*) So I said to him, "Edmond," I said, "you can't make a women suffer like this with impunity."

Léona And what did he say to that?

Emmeline A foul word.

Madame Hortense (*turning on the Pianist as she continues her rounds*) Monsieur Léon in the clouds, as usual! Come along now, quickly. Ready with your *Gay Reverie*, or we shall get all our parts mixed up again! What a dreamer you are! I think your dandruff's getting worse and worse.

Pianist All artists have it.

Madame Hortense Why don't you use the Pope's Lotion I advised you to try?

Pianist It smells oriental. I don't think it's very virile.

Madame Hortense (*with a smile*) When I was with Monsieur Hortense, he used to use it. And I flatter myself that in all our twelve years of marriage I was the best loved woman in the world. Monsieur Hortense performed three times a day—once in the afternoon. Ah! How he spoiled me!

Pianist (*modestly*) He was a violinist, and violinists are . . .

Madame Hortense (*significantly*) I've also known pianists with a fiery temperament.

Pianist (*still modest*) It's rarer, though.

Madame Hortense takes her music back to the heap of sheet music on a table at the back of the stage. Suzanne Délicias leaves her cello and goes over to the piano

Suzanne Délicias She never stops, does she?

Pianist We were just chatting.

Suzanne Délicias If you don't shut her up, I will.

Pianist It's difficult to stop her while customers are here. After all, she's the leader, isn't she?

Suzanne Délicias Coward! Coward! (*She sits down again*)

Patricia (*continuing a conversation with Pamela of which we have not heard the beginning*) Then I rub it with a bit of Kleenall and a really dry, soft rag.

Pamela I prefer a drop of ammonia.

Patricia (*acid*) Ammonia removes the varnish, not the mark.

Pamela (*also aggressive*) Each to her own method.

Patricia Yes, but some methods are bad. Certain women have no pride in their homes.

Pamela My home looks just as good as yours. (*With a laugh*) May be there aren't so many little mats and table runners and things.

Patricia Well, not everyone has artistic taste, I mean, have they? I like my little soft, warm nest, with all my souvenirs around me. The mats and things make it cosy.

Pamela Dust traps. My little place is modern, I'm proud to say. Tubular furniture and formica surfaces. Everything neat and bright. No ornaments.

Patricia (*with a nervous little sneer*) Oh, I can just see it—a clinic. I'm not an invalid.

Madame Hortense changes the number and passes the music around

Pamela And I *am*, I suppose?

Patricia Well, with those eyes . . .

Pamela My eyes may be a little haggard, my dear, but that's because I have a lover who adores me, and that's more than you can say. At least both *my* eyes look in the same direction.

Patricia (*squinting nervously*) Oh! What a thing to say about a physical handicap. Anyway, its hardly noticeable. How low can you sink? And as for your lover, there's no need to boast about him. A bottle-washer!

Pamela (*laughing quite good-naturedly*) One does what one can. The great thing is to make a good job of it. I like a job well done. (*She is cooing insolently*)

Patricia You're unspeakable. I wonder women like you are tolerated in a respectable orchestra.

Madame Hortense Ladies! No arguments on the platform, please Even when we stop playing, the customers don't stop looking. Smiles, please, charm. You can still say what you think with a smile. Your flower, Pamela.

Pamela What about my flower?

Madame Hortense It's drooping. I want all your roses looking fresh!

Patricia (*bitchily*) Like their wearers!

Pamela stamps angrily on Patricia's toe

Ouch!

Madame Hortense Ladies!

Patricia Little bitch! She trod on my toe!

Madame Hortense (*still smiling, but with a glint in her eye*) Manners now, whatever happens. You belong to your public. That's the rule. The manager said to me at the audition, when we got the job in preference to Mag's Star and the Symphony Band—and you know they're both reputable orchestras—he said, "I'm taking you because I want women and charm! An orchestra that will catch my customers' imagination."

Patricia Some hopes of catching imagination in a spa for the cure of constipation. Do you think they listen to us? They talk about it all the time. And tot up their bills. Some bills, too!

Madame Hortense It's not our concern what the customer is thinking, or whether or not he is constipated. Poise and elegance That's what we were engaged for. And quantities of femininity. Now we're going to play *Impressions of Autumn* by Chandoisy, in the Goldstein arrangement. Lots of feeling and vibrato, if you please. (*She slides a finger in passing under Monsieur Léon's collar*) Oh, Monsieur Léon, how warm you are! Your collar is quite damp.

Pianist I always bring two with me. I'll change during the intermission, after the March from *Tannhäuser*.

Suzanne Délicias (*beside herself*) Stop it, stop it! Or I shall leave the platform.

Pianist (*pitifully*) Please, don't let's have a scene. She said I was too warm. I can't very well tell her I'm not.

Suzanne Délicias Monster! You're a monster of cruelty!

Madame Hortense (*very much in command*) Careful of that sharp in the reprise during your solo, Mademoiselle Délicias, won't you, please?

Emmeline (*finishing a conversation with Léona*) Everything! Everything! I told him everything! The rent not paid, my trouble with my poor mother, my period not coming . . .

Léona So what did he say?

Emmeline Nothing. He was asleep.

Léona Well! What an oaf! I'd never have stood that from André.

Madame Hortense taps discreetly with her bow on her double bass.

*The music starts up. Very tender and tuneful. During the perfor-
mance, at chosen points in the music, the musicians talk as they play*

Patricia I'm a woman. I'm probably more of a woman than you,
even though I don't throw myself on my back for anyone that
happens along. I'm waiting for someone—someone I can—I
want to be able to look deep down into his eyes.
Pamela (*puffing out her cheeks as she plays*) You'll have difficulty
doing that with both eyes at once.
Patricia (*stifling a sob at this second jab*) Oh!
Pamela He'll have to change sides from time to time.
Patricia (*another sob*) Oh! It's too much!

Madame Hortense gives her a discreet tap on the head with her bow

*She swallows her emotion and plays with a passionate abandon.
Music*

Emmeline (*continuing*) So then when we went into the restaurant,
an extremely smart place where his friends had invited us, I said
to him: "Where shall I sit, Edmond?"
Léona And what did he say?
Emmeline (*sniffing indignantly*) He said, sit where you f . . .

*A tap on the head from Madame Hortense's bow cuts the word off
just as by general consent the orchestra has drowned it. The piece
comes to an end with much pathos and brilliance of technique. Once
it is over, Madame Hortense collects the music and changes the
number*

Patricia Why is the waiter hanging about with our refreshment ?
I'm dying of thirst. We have some rights!
Pamela (*good-naturedly joining in*) He has customers to serve, so
our glass of beer can wait, needless to say.
Patricia Artistes don't count of course.
Madame Hortense (*changing the number*) During the intermission,
ladies. You know that's the usual thing. We have a right to
refreshments during the intermission.
Patricia Yesterday they served us at midnight. Oh, he's quicker
off the mark on Saturdays, he gets a tip. This week I shall give
him ten centimes. What a life among all these yokels. Some
people find it quite natural, of course, to the point of taking

them to bed. I was brought up differently. An officer's daughter in a clip joint?

Madame Hortense (*vexed*) The Brasserie du Globe et du Portugal is a first-class establishment and you were very lucky to get in, my dear. Don't spit in your own soup.

Patricia And with gifts! Let me tell you, I've played at concerts and I've given recitals. Once at a charity affair, Massenet, the great Massenet, was in the audience. At the end of the concert, he kissed my hand. I had been rendering an arrangement of something by Mignon. I'd really put the whole of myself into it. The Master had tears in his eyes. He was so moved, he could find nothing to say to me. Such an eloquent talker, too. Obviously, you wouldn't understand.

Madame Hortense We all have our little successes. Monsieur Hortense was once first violin at the Brasserie Zurki in Saint Petersburg. I am speaking of the time before the revoloution. He used to play to crowned heads. But there are always ups and downs. It didn't prevent him from doing his job conscientiously He would say to me, "Zélie, music is like greens, it is always good for you."

Patricia Giving all you have to the constipated!

Madame Hortense Constipation never prevented anyone from appreciating music. Just the contrary, I should say. We have some splendid music lovers here. Only yesterday a big Belgian industrialist came over to congratulate me. As a matter of fact, he mentioned you.

Patricia (*suddenly transformed*) Really? How amusing. What did he say?

Madame Hortense He asked me if you came from Ghent. It seems you remind him of someone from there. In charge of the cloakroom at the *Kursaal*.

Emmeline (*continuing to Léona*) So I said to him, "Edmond, maybe *you* don't like it, but don't put other people off!"

Léona Just like that?

Emmeline Just like that. Short and to the point. And then I said, "I'm a woman, and you'll never stop a woman thinking and feeling like a woman." That, my dear, that little pay-off line went right home, I could see that.

Léona What did he say?

Emmeline Nothing. He just went on brushing his teeth.

Léona So what did you do?

Emmeline I put down my scissors—I was cutting my toenails at the time—and went out of the bathroom.

Léona Just like that?

Emmeline Just like that. You've got to admit he didn't get away with that! I put on my girdle and stockings. Still not a word, my dear. He was rinsing his teeth. So I put on my dress. I'd made up my mind. You know me. And I just went out and slammed the door. I was in a rage! The first man, I assure you, the first man to be nice to me I was going to give myself to. Only there was nobody but the night watchman—an old Negro—and you know what Moulins is like in the morning! Not so much as a cat in sight. I walked as far as I could, just to frighten him. I went to have a look at the cathedral since everyone says it's so nice, but there was nothing to look at, and at a quarter past two I went back up. I'd had enough. I had those pink shoes on—the ones I gave you because they were too small and hurt my corns. And anyway, I'd shouted out when I left that we'd have to put an end to it once and for all, so I was afraid he might be frightened of the water and call the police.

Léona Is he frightened of water, then?

Emmeline Don't be so stupid—there's a river running through Moulins. It's the first thing anybody thinks of in the state I was in—everyone knows that. I did go as far as the edge, too, but it was too dark, so I came back.

Léona Oh, I see! He thought you were dead! So what did he say when he saw you?

Emmeline Nothing. He didn't see me. He'd gone out, too.

Léona To fetch the police?

Emmeline No. To have a round with his pals at the allnight bar opposite the station.

Suzanne Délicias (*standing near the piano*) I've put up with everything! Our secret rendezvous, our occasional meetings in that filthy little hotel where the manager talks to me as if I were a tart—me! Who has always dreamed of the day when I could go around with my head held high and be seen arm in arm with the man I love! But there is one thing I won't put up with, Léon—the advances of that horrible woman to the man I've chosen and given myself to! Your poor, sick wife—that's another matter; I can understand pity even if I do find it cowardly and despise the degrading precautions you take. But here, under my very nose, this exhibition of lust! Right here, in the orchestra!

Pianist Our relations are strictly limited to professional matters, my love.

Suzanne Délicias Her finger round your collar just now—was that a professional matter? And what about when she ruffled your hair?

Pianist She was drawing my attention to the dandruff on the collar of my jacket. It was strictly her professional right as director of the orchestra.

Suzanne Délicias (*trembling*) Your collar is mine, Léon, your hair is mine, even your dandruff is mine! I'm the only one who should be worrying about that little snowstorm! I'm the one who should be brushing your collar! I've given you everything—my saved-up virginity, my illusions, the good name of an irreproachable family—and then there's my religious sister, who'd die if she heard of this. Everything you are is mine now! I shall claw at her like a she-lion!

Madame Hortense passes near Suzanne Délicias

Pianist (*mildly*) Lionesses bite. It's tigresses that claw—I've told you before, my love.

Suzanne Délicias Right! Then I'll bite! (*As Madame Hortense passes near her, she suddenly shows her teeth with a lion-like roar as though she is about to take a bite at her*) Rrrr-rr-rr!

Madame Hortense (*halting*) Is something the matter?

Suzanne Délicias bursts into sobs

Pianist (*stammering*) It's just nerves. Just nerves.

Madame Hortense Nerves or no nerves, my dear, *not* on the platform! We're the centre of attention of the entire establishment. (*To Léon*) You! Give her a slap on the back; they'll think she was choking. We don't want a scandal in the orchestra!

Pianist (*doing so*) My little lamb, my little bunny rabbit, my little stoat . . .

Madame Hortense Now, now. The *Fables* of La Fontaine can wait. During off hours, I don't care how you pass the time, the two of you!

Suzanne Délicias (*to Léon, irritably*) Stop slapping me like that.

You're hurting. (*To Madame Hortense, pulling herself up*) I'm
in love and I'm loved, if you want to know, madame!

Madame Hortense No, Mademoiselle Délicias. No. I do not want
to know. We are in the temple of music here.

Suzanne Délicias Oh no, that's too easy—trying to shut me up in
the name of Art. Do you think I'm ashamed? I can hold my head
up! Yes I can hold my head up! (*She does so on the platform for
a ridiculously long interval*)

Madame Hortense (*snatching the music Suzanne Délicias is
brandishing*) All I ask of you is that you don't ruin your music
sheet. Don't you realize what it costs, this music? Just look at
that. *Cockades and Cock-crows* all crumpled up. And it's an
extremely rare piece!

Suzanne Délicias (*with a contemptuous laugh*) Extremely rare—
really, your taste for cheap music is deplorable, if I may say so,
Madame Hortense. Extremely rare! Duverger!

Madame Hortense Arranged by Benoisseau, my dear! And he was
a man who knew his job. I'm sorry I have to tell you that. I
knew him at the Casino de Royan, in the good old days of the
Symphony Orchestra. There was a musician for you!

Suzanne Delicias I was brought up on the classics. Ah, Beethoven,
Saint-Saëns . . . !

Madame Hortense In a place like this, the customer plays cards or
dominoes to forget his health troubles. What he wants is a good
backround noise. This piece is gay, vibrant, lively. And it
makes one think of France—that's always a good thing in a
café.

Suzanne Délicias Oh, I've sunk too low! All these humiliations
will kill me! Such mediocrity—it's suffocating. I shan't sing the
great aria from *La Vestale*. My voice is broken. I'm in no condi-
tion to sing.

Madame Hortense (*severely*) The aria from *La Vestale* is on the
programme. It's in print. A change of programme always makes
a bad impression. Monsieur Lebonze has absolutely forbidden it
It confuses his customers. You will sing it.

Suzanne Délicias (*sitting down suddenly, groaning*) No! No! This is
too much. It's too much for my nerves. Help me, Léon! This
woman is persecuting me!

Madame Hortense You are a small person. Monsieur Léon is a
man and an artist. He will be obliged to agree with me. (*She*

continues on her Olympian way, distributing the music to the members of the orchestra)

Emmeline I'm saying nothing. It's not my lookout. But if anyone took it into their heads to take a tenth of the liberties with Edmond that she takes with that unfortunate boy, I should see red. Once at the casino at Palavas, I go out for a moment during the interval. When I come back, he's not on the platform. You know where I find him?

Léona No.

Emmeline With the lavatory attendant.

Leona No!

Emmiline Oh yes. A blonde creature with a horrible reputation. Can you imagine? A pee-pee girl!

Léona What was he doing?

Emmeline He pretended afterward that he was asking her for some change, but he couldn't fool me. You know what I said to him?

Léona No.

Emmeline Nothing. I just looked at them, like that, said, "Is there any paper?" and walked straight into the Ladies'.

Léona Just like that. And what did he do?

Emmeline He went into the Gents', without a word. But let me tell you, he had turned quite pale. I could see he'd taken the snub.

Léona You did quite right. Some people have to be put in their place.

Madame Hortense (*suddenly, from the back*) Men! I've had dozens of them? Tall ones, handsome ones, well-set-up ones. Since Monsieur Hortense died, I've been taking a rest. But I just want you to know that if I needed one . . .!

Suzanne Délicias May one know what would happen if you needed one, madame?

Madame Hortense I would choose a better-built one—there!

Suzanne Délicias Léon is beautiful. He has a Grecian nose.

Madame Hortense Grecian nose or no Grecian nose, I couldn't care less. I believe in a chest measurement.

Pianist Ladies!

Madame Hortense Monsieur Hortense was a wardrobe of a man. He crushed a women in bed. That's love for you!

Suzanne Délicias How crude you are, madame.

Pianist Ladies!

Suzanne Délicias Keep your stevedores, your waiters, your brutes
—I despise them. I vomit them! I'd die rather than let them
come near me with their great fists. Léon has an Apollo's figure.
Not a trace of a stomach. Show her, Léon! I will not have
people say you aren't beautiful.

Pianist (*horrified*) Suzanne! Not in the orchestra!

Suzanne Délicias (*atremble*) Why not? I'm proud of our love! I
want to brave everybody and their opinions—I want to brave
the entire world!

Madame Hortense (*who has suddenly cast a terrified look at the end
of the room*) Suzanne Délicias, the manager is looking at us.
You know he won't have gossiping in the orchestra. And our
contract is renewable every two weeks. (*She calls out obse-
quiously*) Right away, Monsieur Lebonze, right away! We're off!
Are you ready ladies? *Cockades and Cock-crows.* Smartly now.
Very lively. Let's go, now—one, two, three, four . . . .

*The orchestra, everyone having scuttled back to position, attacks
the glossy, heroic music. Suzanne Délicias is muttering to herself
meanwhile as she plays furiously on her cello*

Suzanne Délicias I shall kill myself.

Pianist (*groaning as he plays*) Suzanne.

Suzanne Délicias With laudanum.

Pianist (*as before but with a different tone of voice each time*)
Suzanne.

Music

Suzanne Délicias I shall go and throw myself in the river.

Pianist (*distracted*) Suzanne.

Suzanne Délicias Or under a train.

Pianist Suzanne.

*With music still playing, Suzanne suddenly bursts in to derisive
laughter*

Suzanne Délicias Not likely! That's just what she'd like. She'd
have you at last! You know what I'm going to do tomorrow?
I'm going to buy myself a new dress. The most expensive I can
find at Petit Paris. I'll blow two weeks' pay on it and make her
mad with my wasp waist—showing up her great, fat, undignified
backside!

Pianist Suzanne!

Suzanne Délicias (*demands suddenly*) Do you love me, Léon?

Pianist I adore you, my love. I shall never love anyone but you.

Suzanne Délicias You're not afraid of death?

Pianist With you!

Suzanne Délicias (*beside herself*) Yes!

Pianist (*with conviction*) No!

Suzanne Délicias So we shall die together if we are too unhappy. We'll have them fooled.

Pianist (*lukewarm*) Quite.

Suzanne Délicias (*gloomily, over her cello, while the music becomes more and more spirited*) It's good to die!

Pianist (*halfhearted*) Delicious!

A flourish of chords as the music comes to an end. Applause here and there throughout the room. Madame Hortense, delighted, acknowledges it discreetly and gestures towards the orchestra with her hand. Madame Hortense goes around collecting the music

Madame Hortense You heard the way they applauded. So *Cockades and Cock-crows* arranged by Benoisseau is still cheap music, mm? What a reaction, my dears, what a reaction! Did you see that? That piece really penetrates the vitals! The Frenchman knows that it was written for him. (*She throws this remark at Suzanne*) You have turnip juice in your veins and no love for your country not to feel what that music has to give!

Suzanne Délicias My answer to that is utter contempt!

Madame Hortense Now I have patriotism in my blood! During the war at the height of unemployment, I refused a season at Vichy. And I know some who wouldn't have had any scruples. Even played for the enemy!

Suzanne Délicias Your insinuations leave me cold as marble. It is true that I played in a Paris brasserie in nineteen forty but it was a resistance orchestra. Whenever there were German officers in the place, the word went around to play out of tune. That needed some courage! We could have been denounced—those people were all musicians!

Madame Hortense (*laughing unpleasantly*) Knowing you, I should think playing out of tune came all too easily!

Suzanne Délicias (*pulling herself up, pale*) Oh, this is too much! If you're going to insult my art, if nothing's to be sacred here, I'm leaving . . .

Suzanne gets up and leaves the platform. The pianist, deathly pale, runs and catches her as she goes out

Patricia (*to Pamela*) There, you see! She's going too far attacking her that way. Maybe she didn't play at Vichy, but she played over the radio.

Pianist (*at floor level with Suzanne, whom he is trying to deter*) This argument is ridiculous, like all arguments. Nobody's questioning your talent, Suzanne!

Suzanne Délicias (*with a bitter laugh*) To hell with my talent! It's always possible I didn't even have that! And I thought I was making such a gift of myself! It's too funny. Don't you find it funny? So I've given nothing to Art, or to my country, or to you.

Pianist (*wearily*) No, you haven't . . . I mean, yes you have! Now, please, Suzanne, don't let's have a scandal!

Suzanne Délicias I'm beyond scandal now. I've been putting up for a long time, Léon. I've given myself to degrading conditions in furnished hotels! (*Shouting madly*) *Furnished* hotels!

Pianist (*stammering pitifully*) Quiet, now, Suzanne, quiet. Hotels are always furnished—in Europe at least—and, anyway, when we were travelling . . .

Suzanne Délicias (*with a prolonged nervous laugh*) Oh yes, when we were travelling. Never got very far, though, did we? The other side of town—on foot! We were the sort of travellers who really didn't need luggage! I've suffered enough. Oh, the way the manager would look at me when we asked for our room, the look he gave me—sharing me with you in advance.

Pianist You exaggerate, Suzanne. He's a respectable married man. . .

Suzanne Délicias (*contemptuous*) That makes two of you—respectable married men—sharing me on my so very short travels! We made love with an eye on the time, Léon, so that your so dear and so pathetic invalid wife shouldn't go mad with your everlasting late home-comings. What about me—wasn't I as pathetic and ill as she was?

Pianist It wasn't the same thing, Suzanne!

Suzanne Délicias (*with rising excitement*) Maybe we were travel-

ling without baggage, but we did have watches. One each, on the
bedside tables. Some lovers lie and play at listening to each
other's hearts, to see if they beat in time. But we spent our time
in bed checking whether we had the right time by our watches.
Oh, that watch, that watch, I hate it. (*She throws it on the floor
and stamps on it*) I'm throwing it out; I'm stamping on it! Give
me yours! (*She tries to snatch his watch*)

Pianist (*a pathetic figure, defending his own watch as he picks up the
other*) My love, the whole place can see us! The glass isn't
broken, fortunately. You're exaggerating, Suzanne. Everyone
watches out for the time these days. Modern life is lived with an
eye on the clock . . .

Suzanne Délicias Oh yes, I've lived modern life all right. I've been
a free woman, liberated from prejudice as they say. But they're
in chains all the same, these free women. All tied up in watch
chains! I've been a free woman weighed down with watch chains
Isn't that amusing?

Pianist I told you at the start that I couldn't risk killing my poor
sick wife. And you told me our love would be so great!

Suzanne Délicias (*still ridiculous, but with a sort of sincere misery*)
Well, it wasn't—it wasn't big enough! It was murdered, murdered with the hands of a watch. It got drowned in the lavatory
bowl along with the children I could have had. Ten times I
suggested we should kill ourselves, Léon. Dying together would
have been clean! To drown the lot once for all: father, mother,
and children, instead of just children. That would have been
simple!

Pianist (*stammering*) It only seemed simple, my love. I had no
right to leave her either. . .

Suzanne Délicias (*shouting*) But me, you had the right to leave me
at the end of my daily three-quarters of an hour. I was a
ridiculous old maid and I'd waited all that time just to be a
woman three quarters of an hour a day! To the minute. Timed
on two watches, if you please!

Pianist (*correcting her idiotically*) An hour! An hour and a half!
I'd told my wife I had to be on here a good hour later—you
know that!

Suzanne Délicias (*also idiotic, but somehow touching as well*) Yes,
but there was all that walking! And I only had the right to be
your wife on the other side of town. Someone might have seen

us otherwise. We had to be good and just walk side by side—as though we didn't know each other!

Pianist (*trying to be romantic*) What did it matter, so long as we loved each other! Does time count?

Suzanne Délicias (*serious*) Yes, I've finally decided that it counts terribly. And that's just what life is made of. (*Stating*) I've wasted my time. Funny expression, isn't it? Wasted my time. No good praying to Saint Anthony to give it back to me. (*She suddenly bursts out*) What time do you make it, Léon? Do we both make it the same? My watch says a quarter to eleven.

Pianist (*mechanically consulting his*) Mine says quarter to twelve. We should be playing, Suzanne. Get up on the platform. We'll talk about it during the intermission—my love. We'll have a long quarter of an hour to ourselves.

Suzanne Délicias (*haughtily*) Thanks. I've already finished here.

Madame Hortense (*in a low voice*) Now, have we finished with this scene? The manager's looking at us. Do you want to have us all thrown out? That's what your trying to do, isn't it, you little sourpuss?

Suzanne Délicias (*dignified*) No, madame. So far as I am concerned, I'm out already. I refuse once and for all to play out of tune. Good-bye, madame. I leave him to you. But you were right—he's a runt. (*She turns haughtily*) I hope you have a good watch at least?

Suzanne bursts into a long, nervous laugh, and exits

Madame Hortense (*calling after her*) You'll get five hundred francs' fine, my girl. And I warn you, you'll be replaced on Saturday!

Pianist (*returning to the platform, head lowered*) She's suffering, Madame Hortense. You are abusing your power. (*He groans as he sits down at his pathetic piano*) You should be ashamed.

Madame Hortense It's you who should be ashamed, Monsieur Léon, with your poor, sick wife. That hysterical creature will end up telling her everything to relieve her own feelings.

Pianist (*desperately*) It's too much—too much!

Madame Hortense I know men, Monsieur Léon. I've managed other men besides you. A man has need of contentment, it's only human. No one will reproach you for that, in your situation. But entrust yourself to a proper woman, who knows what life is and who will have something to give. I was lying just now, I don't find you skinny at all. A little slender perhaps, but for someone motherly, like me, that's just one of your charms. (*She passes a finger around his collar again*) Oh! how warm he is, how warm he is, the wicked man. And he doesn't like being petted. He does so need someome to look after him.

Pianist (*weeping, his head in her arms*) These scenes destroy my nerves. I'm an artist. I'm not made for real life.

Madame Hortense We'll help you, we'll help you, my dear. I understand you so well. Why the need for scenes over every little thing? A little discreet pleasure—shouldn't that be enough to make for happiness? You're swimming. Change your collar my poppet.

Pianist (*broken but heroic*) After the March from *Tannhäuser*. No point in doing it before. (*He snivels*) You mustn't think I don't still love my wife. Twelve years—you can't forget that so easily I could have put her in a home. She's incurable. Who would have blamed me? I've kept her at home, in spite of her insane jealousy. I've taken a housekeeper, a woman I can rely on. But all that costs money. Sometimes I feel so alone.

Madame Hortense You should have someone to help you instead of torturing you even more. That's all there is to it. Someone sensitive, like yourself.

Pianist (*groaning*) I'm a harp. It takes nothing to break me.

Madame Hortense You are an artist. And artists don't need emotions outside their art. A little pleasure, yes. That's all. The rest goes into music. Haven't you noticed that that mad creature was the only one who caused us any trouble in the orchestra?

Pianist She's a harp too!

Madame Hortense Yes, but a broken-down harp. Leaving the orchestra like that, just for a whim! Just when we ought to be striking up *Cuban Delights*. Léona, be a good girl and go and see what's she's doing, the little lunatic. She's probably sniveling away in the toilets!

Léona exits

Sentiment is all very fine, but we have a job to do. We're in danger of losing our engagement as well. The manager's on the prowl. I don't know what's the matter with him this evening, he's so suspicious. (*She begins to busy herself with the parts*)

Patricia (*pursuing a sudden friendly conversation with Pamela*) All the same, she was absolutely horrible to her. First of all, people should stop talking about the war. I resisted, like anyone else. I listened to London radio every day. I did what I could. But I had my poor old mother. I had to see she had some comforts.

Pamela Does your old girl still live with you?

Patricia (*with a sour little laugh*) Sure. Poor Toots. That's what I call her. She's my baby now. I've decided to devote my life entirely to her. To her and my art. There's nothing else I can do with such a small place.

Pamela You know, I just couldn't do it. When I go to see mine at Batignolles—she's not badly off, she's a concierge—it's all right for a while: "Hullo, Maman. How are you, Maman? I'm all right, Maman." Makes me feel like a kid again. There'll be Irish stew waiting for me—it's her favourite vice, Irish stew. But by the third mouthful, without fail we start bawling each other out. The plates start jumping around the table and off I go home again.

Patricia (*smiling slightly*) You mustn't think we don't have our little skirmishes, too, poor Toots and me. As she gets older, she more and more like a little girl. Whims and fancies every turn. Oh, but I'm very severe with her! When she goes to steal a sweet, the rascal, smack! A good rap on the knuckles for her. "Ooh! Ooh!" she snivels, but after that, she's good. It's obviously boredom that accounts for all these little yearnings. And then again I've tried to train her to "ask", but it's no good; the wicked old thing always dirties herself.

Pamela It's just a phase. It'll probably adjust itself in time.

Patricia She's getting on for eighty, so I don't hold out much hope any more. But there again I've decided to be absolutely inflexible. I change her three times a day, and if she forgets herself meanwhile, so much the worse for her. I often think she does it out of spite, you know. Sometimes, when I'm all rigged out ready to leave for work, she'll call out "caca" and start whimpering. My goodness—that's just too bad! I leave her until midnight to lie in her own mess. That teaches her.

Pamela You have to be firm with them. My girl, when I had her with me . . .

Patricia (*cutting in*) And you know what she's been trying ever since last winter? She's started sucking her thumb!

Pamela My mother used to smear mustard on mine, but I don't what you'd do with old people.

Patricia Mustard? She'd be only too happy! She adores mustard. She adores anything that's bad for her. Oh, if I were to let her eat what she wants! Any time I find her at it, she gets a jolly good rap. And no pudding. That's where it hurts most. Oh, the puddings and sweets she'd have if I let her—all my pills would disappear, even! But I'm very firm about that. No sweets or sugary things in the house. If a visitor brings any, I hide them, and she can have one a week, on Sundays, if she's been good. You should hear the blubbering at the cupboard when I take them away from her. "Sweetie! Sweetie!" Just like a baby.

Pamela It's for their own good. They'd only get toothache.

Patricia (*with the same sour little smile*) Poor Toots! She hasn't got any teeth any more. But it's the principle of the thing, you see. Once you start giving way to them . . .

Pamela It can't be much fun having that sort of thing every day.

Patricia (*gravely*) There's a great satisfaction in knowing one's duty. *Maman* is everything to me, apart from my art. And I make the sacrifice cheerfully. Believe me, and I think I can say this without boasting, I am a model daughter. It's just that she must be straight with me.

Pamela I sent my daughter away to the country. What with my work and being separated from my husband, I just couldn't. And then you know, I'm a real woman, I need men, And men can never get used to the child. And even if one did come along by chance who got used to her, you know how it is sooner or later he'd change. Anyway, all I have goes for her clothes. I want her to be a real coquette, my Mouquette, a real little woman, I want her to be. On her fifth birthday I gave her a really sophisticated dress. Silk, you know, with the hooped petticoat and the ribbons —twelve thousand francs it cost me. You can see I'm not stingy over her. And I sent her some money for a perm and some nail varnish and lipstick. She looked so sweet! You should have seen her with her little nails painted and her lips made up and everything. What a love! Me all over, she looked, my dear. That's what I adore about her. She's the absolute image of me. It was too bad I couldn't stay. I had a tiff with Fernand. He wouldn't get out of the car and kept sounding the horn continuously out in the street. And there she was calling out, "*Maman, Maman,* you haven't even given me a proper kiss." (*She sighs*) It would be nice to see more of them! But what can you do? Life's like that. Anyway, she had her party frock. She'll remember that, later on.

Patricia When you're an artiste, you have heart. My friends keep telling me I should put her in a home, where she'd have all the attention she needs, poor Toots. True, she'd be better off than at home, where she's nearly always alone on account of my work. But I really couldn't . . . I'd rather correct her firmly when she's naughty and know I've done my duty. She's my mother. My friends say, "You're a saint, Patricia," but I always say, "You never recover your losses!" The only thing I ask of her is that she's grateful. Otherwise, a good smack and no pudding.

Pamela But, you know, if you do recover them, you don't do so well! I could have stayed with her father and kept her. He found me with Georges, but he thought it was the first time. These things happen in any family and it gets forgotten, especially if there's a child. But Georges said he was leaving for Nice, and at the beginning I thought I couldn't do without the man. I was crazy about him. So I left the child. Mind you, two months later we parted, but how was I to know? That's life!

Patricia Maybe your husband would have taken you back?

Pamela I thought about that, mostly because of the child. The divorce wasn't through and with that man I had only to appear and everything would have been settled in bed. So I packed my things and went back. But I met someone in the train—I was in funds at the time and had treated myself to first class—we were alone in the compartment. You know how it is! Ah! Night trains, my dear, they should be forbidden. (*She sighs*) And to think I'd bought her the dearest little regional costume from Nice, with the matching hat and skirt—well, anyway, I had to send it to her. She must have been thrilled with it, my little Mouquette. Apparently her friends at school were sick with envy. The kid told me in a letter that the other girls had said, "You're in luck, having a mother like that." Imagine—I'd bought her the prettiest model, with the apron in real silk. There's nothing I wouldn't do for my kid!

Léona enters

Léona I've looked everywhere, she's not in the toilets. There's one that's engaged, but I didn't dare bang on the door. I was afraid it might be a client.

Madame Hortense Bitch! Never mind! Lets tackle *Cuban Delights* just the same. Monsieur Lebonze has just looked at his watch. He must be thinking we're taking our time. Emmeline, be so kind as to leave your instrument and take the cello part. He may not notice the gap so much that way.

Emmeline What does he know about music?

Madame Hortense Nothing, but he can count. And there are only six of us now. We'll tell him she had food poisoning. It happened last week to a customer who ate the wrong sort of mushroom.

Léona helps Emmeline to the other seat. Madame Hortense distributes the parts

Emmeline She's suffering, that girl. I can understand it only too well—love's a killer. Once I told Edmond, right to his face, "Edmond," I said, "sentiment forgives nothing. If I find you with another woman, I shall shut my eyes and pull the trigger. A woman who has suffered what I have suffered—there are laws in this country—I'll get off."

Pianist So what did he say?

Emmeline Nothing. But he was yawning at the time. So he stopped and picked up the paper.

Léona Just like that.

Emmeline Just like that. I could see it had gone home.

Madame Hortense Now, off we go. I want this very warm—very sensual.

Madame Hortense taps discreetly on her music stand with her bow. She gives them one bar before starting and the orchestra then launches into "Cuban Delights," a syncopated piece heavy with sensuality. They have put on appropriate headgear and are throwing themselves heart and soul into their playing. Léona has left her flute for an exotic instrument. The piece has a refrain which everyone sings quietly as they play. It is a tradition. It suddenly makes itself heard during the muted passage at the second reprise

Orchestra (*singing*) Delights, delights, Cuban delights! In Cuba, in Cuba! Delights, delights in Cuba!

Music

Pamela (*to Patricia, hollowly*) This tune makes me feel quite peculiar. It's silly it should be so evocative!

Patricia (*sourly, as she plays*) Cheap music.

Pamela Yes, but it reminds you of love. You wouldn't understand my dear. But when you have men in your blood, the way I have ... Take Georges, for example. Oh! How I missed that man He beat me and he was stupid, so stupid—a real moron. But in bed ... After all, what is there to say to each other during the day, anyway? Have you really never made love not even once?

Patricia There are questions one woman should never even ask another. I told you I've given everything to my art, and to poor Toots!

Music

Orchestra Delights, delights—Cuban delights! Etc.

Madame Hortense (*to the Pianist, in a hollow whisper*) For one thing the girl is a skinny creature anyway. You need flesh for love-making. For small men like you, Monsieur Léon, the woman has to take care of you, wrap you around; men like you have to be kept warm, they must be able to bury themselves in the woman, hide themselves in her!

Pianist (*groaning suddenly*) Oh, Mother, Mother! *Maman* was the only one who loved me!

Madame Hortense I'll be your *maman*, my chicken! You shall bury yourself in my bosom. Skinny women only think of themselves. They have nothing to give.

Pianist Oh, *Maman!*

Orchestra (*singing*) Delights, delights, Cuban delights! Etc.

Patricia (*mournfully*) Don't think I don't suffer! Sometimes when I'm undressing I look at myself in the glass. I'm beautiful! Really beautiful! My figure is nice and round and my legs are smooth, but I just can't!

Pamela It's not so difficult!

Music

Orchestra (*singing*) Delights, delights . . .

Emmeline (*to Léona*) But, you know, Edmond's a real boor. I've never, but never, known such a pig. Never a kind word. Nothing. Dumb and clumsy as a carp!

Léona A bull!

Emmeline But he's part of me. When that part's taken away, I'm not complete any more and there's nothing for it but to wait until he wants to come back—to finish me off, if you understand what I mean?

Léona It's quite clear. It's no longer his, it's yours.

Emmeline That's why he'll get those six bullets in his head if he ever gets the idea of taking himself off with anyone! Bang, bang, bang, bang, bang, bang!

Léona Just like that.

Emmeline That's love.

Music

Orchestra Delights, delights, Cuban delights! Etc.

The piece comes to an end. Increasing applause. The pianist, still wearing his Mexican hat, suddenly turns on the piano like a hunted animal and shouts

Pianist I do not give a damn! My wife weeping away all the time in that armchair—and the other one as well with tears and her emotions! Damn them both! (*He shouts wildly*) Damn them! It's torture crying with both of them, suffering twice over! Once in the hotel room without any clothes and again at home fully dressed. I'm getting thin, losing weight, pining away; I've got acid stomach with it all, but deep down inside me I've got to admit I don't give a damn! Sometimes I slip away all by myself and go down to the river where they've got that bathing place and I look at them, all those women in bikinis offering themselves to the sun. I look sort of preoccupied and you'd probably think I was just going for a walk, or looking for someone, but it's not true. I'm not looking for anyone. *I'm* the sun. I'm taking them—I'm taking the lot of them, one after the other! Slowly, thoroughly! And what's more I ring the changes. Brunettes, blondes, redheads, coloureds, thin, fat, the lot! Just as the mood takes me! Young ones, that haven't got around to it yet, and matrons with rather riper pleasures to offer. And there they all are—spread out, bottoms up—you'd never think they were the same you can see so respectably sipping afternoon tea in the patisserie. There they are offering everything to you with the best will in the world, their beauties and their secrets, offering you every inch of themselves, so as not to miss a single ray of sunshine. The magazines have told them it has to be nicely done all over! (*Shouting with unpleasant laughter*) Done! Done! Done! On the spit! With me as chef! I'm Nero! Tiberius! Farouk! All of them, all of them mine! One after the other—sometimes several at a time! Some of them I'm nice to, stroking them gently and putting some feeling into it. But the others I take the whip to, and some I have killed off afterward! (*He is quite out of breath and exhausted, but he adds lyrically*) With tarts you knew you could have it, but you had to approach them and anyway it's expensive, and there was always the danger of disease, but these "nice" women's rumps, these really luscious ones—who'd have thought we'd have the lot of them one day—all of them for nothing! (*Yelling like a mad thing*) Three cheers for bathing stations! (*Adding sharply, cutting it short*) An enormous Lido and everybody stark naked! Everybody! By law! On pain of death!

Madame Hortense (*terrified*) Monsieur Léon, my poor lamb. You mustn't excite yourself so on duty. Come now, pull yourself together. There's the manager staring at us!

There is suddenly the noise of a pistol shot in the distance. The musicians look up uneasily. There is a flurry, which is quickly stifled

Monsieur Lebonze, the manager, enters majestically, napkin in hand. A waiter runs across the stage

Monsieur Lebonze Who in God's name sent me such an orchestra! Is this what you think you're paid for, you litter of pigs? To go and commit suicide in the firm's toilets? And when we're busy, too. Just to put the customer off, I suppose! I'm sick of your scenes. I shall engage another orchestra tomorrow! Now get going! Play! Play! Bunch of boneheads! Faster! Faster than that! And make it loud—and lively! We don't want the customers suspecting anything.!

Madame Hortense Is she dead?

Monsieur Lebonze How do I know? They're just forcing the door

The doctor's coming. Let's have some music now! God in heaven! Music, immediately! We've told the customers at the other end that the percolator's exploded.

Monsieur Lebonze goes off in the direction of the toilets

Madame Hortense rushes madly around changing the parts. The musicians get hopelessly involved, colliding with one another and knocking over music stands

Madame Hortense Hurry, girls, hurry! We'll have to skip the aria from *La Vestale*. Number seven. We'll have to change the number. Let's take the *Little Marquis Gavotte*. The fool! I said she'd bring us bad luck. What rhyme or reason does it make to kill yourself except to annoy others? Hats on, everyone! Let's make it lively!

The orchestra, distraught, hurl themselves to their seats. They all put on ridiculous little Louis XV hats made of cardboard

Ready! One and two and three and—*Grazioso!*

The orchestra attack the genre piece, which is light and gay, playing it with spirit

The Manager returns

The players make little simpering grimaces under the stern eye of the Manager as they play

The Waiter comes running in, followed by the Doctor

The orchestra continues playing, with many airs and graces, as—

the CURTAIN *falls*

FURNITURE AND PROPERTY LIST

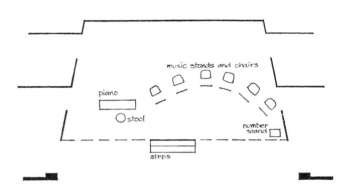

On stage: Piano. *On it:* sheet music, some arranged in piles for distribution

6 music stands with music

Piano stool

6 chairs

Number stand and cards

Instruments: Violin **(Patricia)**

Violin **(Pamela)**

Double bass **(Madame Hortense)**

Cello **(Suzanne Délicias)**

Viola **(Emmeline)**

Flute **(Léona)**

By **Suzanne Délicias's** *chair:* knitting

By each chair: a Cuban or Mexican hat; a cardboard Louis XV hat

Potted palms and other decorative items at discretion

Personal: **Suzanne Délicias:** watch

Pianist: watch

LIGHTING PLOT

Property fittings required: ornamental brackets or chandelier, strip
lights on music stands, all at producer's discretion

To open: General overall stage lighting
No cues

PRINTED IN GREAT BRITAIN BY
THE KINGFISHER PRESS, LONDON NW10